Science in a Flash

States of Matter

Georgia Amson-Bradshaw

Gareth Stevens
PUBLISHING

Please visit our website, www.garethstevens.com.
For a free color catalog of all our high-quality books,
call toll free 1-800-542-2595 or fax 1-877-542-2596.

Cataloging-in-Publication Data

Names: Amson-Bradshaw, Georgia.
Title: States of matter / Georgia Amson-Bradshaw.
Description: New York : Gareth Stevens Publishing, 2018. | Series: Science in a flash | Includes index.
Identifiers: ISBN 9781538214770 (pbk.) | ISBN 9781538214015 (library bound) | ISBN 9781538214787 (6 pack)
Subjects: LCSH: Matter--Juvenile literature. | Matter--Properties--Juvenile literature.
Classification: LCC QC173.16 A47 2018 | DDC 530.4--dc23

Published in 2018 by
Gareth Stevens Publishing
111 East 14th Street, Suite 349
New York, NY 10003

Copyright © 2018 Franklin Watts, a division of Hachette Children's Group

Series Editor: Georgia Amson-Bradshaw
Series Designer: Rocket Design (East Anglia) Ltd

The publisher would like to thank the following for permission to reproduce their pictures: Images from shutterstock:
karpenko_ilia 4tr, 4t, Elvetica 6, MO_SES Premium 8b, ImagePixel 8r, Nenov Brothers Images 9t, hans.slegers 9b,
egg design 10t, TFoxFoto 11tr, Photo Melon 12t, Zilu8 13t, GraphicsRF 14, Javier Brosch 14br, Lorelyn Medina 15,
Vladimir Sazonov 16b, Lucie Lang 17bl, Mamuka Gotsiridze 17br, Artisticco 18, geniuscook_com 20c, Guingm 20bl
Creative Nature Media 22l, Coprid 21cr, Macrovector 23b, GraphicsRF 24b nobeastsofierce 27t Images from other
sources: SecretDisc wiki commons 26b Illustrations by Steve Evans: 5br, 6r, 7l, 11br, 12b, 14bl, 15c, 17t, 18b, 19b,
23br, 25br, 27br. All design elements from Shutterstock.

Printed in China
CPSIA compliance information: Batch CW18GS: For further information
contact Gareth Stevens, New York, New York at 1-800-542-2595.

In this book you'll see
some words shown in **bold**.
They are defined in the
glossary on page 30.

Adult supervision is
required when carrying
out the experiments
in this book.

Contents

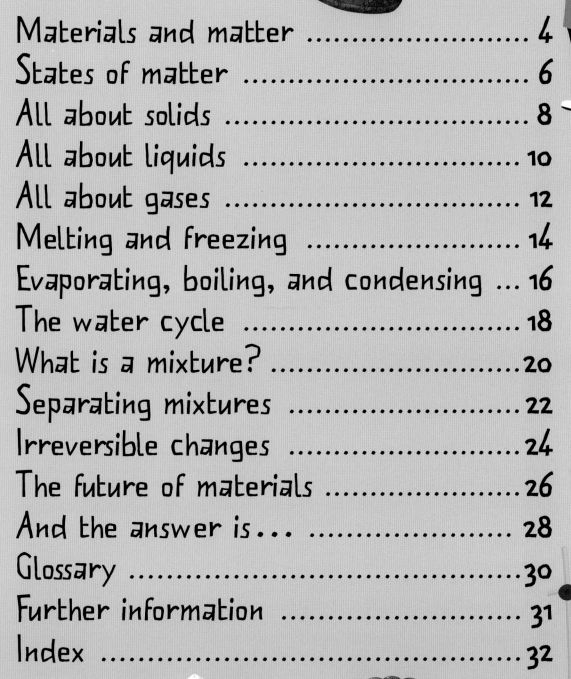

MATERIALS AND MATTER

Everything in the world is made from matter.

Matter is what we call all stuff. If you can feel it, smell it, or taste it, it is matter. Even things you can't see, such as air and other **gases**, are made of matter.

What's the matter?

Everything! It's all matter...

BUILDING BLOCKS

All matter is made up of **atoms**, which are the tiny building blocks of all stuff. If you kept dividing a gold coin into smaller and smaller bits, eventually you would end up with one atom of gold—the smallest bit of gold possible.

GOLD!

MOLECULES

Sometimes atoms join together into groups called **molecules**. Joining atoms into molecules often forms the smallest building block of a new **material**. For example, the smallest building block of water is a single water molecule.

GOLD

GOLD ATOM

WATER

WATER MOLECULE

ZOOM

ZOOM

MATERIAL WORLD

A material is the word for a particular type of matter. Water is a material, and so are rubber, plastic, wood, and steel. Materials can be described by their **properties**, such as hardness, softness, or transparency.

WATER

WOOD

HOUSE

DESIRABLE PROPERTIES

The properties of different materials make them useful for different things. For example, buildings are often made of hard, strong materials to stop them from falling down.

Riddle me this!

Buildings are normally made from hard materials, such as bricks and wood. But buildings in earthquake-prone areas are often built with soft, flexible materials, such as rubber, in their foundations. Why do you think this is?

Answer on page 28.

Did you know?

Diamond is the hardest natural material in the world. The only thing that can scratch a diamond is another diamond!

5

STATES OF MATTER

Matter can be a solid, a liquid, or a gas.

Look around you at the different types of matter and materials that you can see and feel. A **solid** wooden table, perhaps? A glass of water? The air blowing in and out of your lungs? All materials can be divided up into three main **states** of matter: solid, **liquid**, or gas.

Changing states

Some materials can easily change between the three states. For example, water can be a solid (ice), a liquid, or a gas (water vapor). These changes are caused by heating or cooling.

gas
(water vapor)

liquid
(water)

solid (ice)

POP QUIZ!

Which of these is an example of a liquid:

a) Salt

b) Jelly

c) Oil

Answer on page 28.

Cooking with chemistry

We often change the states of materials in the kitchen. We put liquid juice in the freezer to make solid popsicles. We **melt** solid butter into a liquid on the stove to fry things in.

ARGH! Look at the state of your hat!

FACT ATTACK

There is a fourth state of matter called **plasma**, but it is very unusual. It is created when the atoms in a gas start to break down. Plasma television screens contain plasma.

Irreversible changes

Not all materials change back and forth between states like water can. Wood or cotton fabrics that are heated don't become liquid—they **burn**. These sorts of changes are not reversible. Learn more about **irreversible** changes on page 24.

All about solids

Solids keep their shape.

Solid objects are kind of like the sturdy, sensible ones in the bunch—they always keep themselves together and stay in shape. This is because the particles (the atoms or molecules) that make up a solid are very tightly bonded and stick firmly together.

Yeah, I like to stay in shape.

Particles in a solid hold firmly together.

Some materials that are solid are very hard, like brick.

Solid materials can be natural or human-made. Wood is a natural material. Plastic is a human-made material.

Some solids, like butter, are soft and can be squashed into a new shape, but they do not flow.

Solids don't change shape if you turn them upside down or put them into a new container.

Solids have a fixed **volume**. This means they always take up the same amount of space, even if they change shape.

Some solid materials, such as sand, are **powders**. Powders can behave a little differently than other solids. This is because they are made up of lots of tiny pieces of solid material. Each individual piece behaves like a normal solid, but when they are all added together they can flow, like a liquid.

Sponges can seem like they have a smaller volume when they are squashed. But in fact, the solid part of the sponge keeps the same volume. It is air spaces inside the sponge that get pushed out, making it seem smaller.

Did you know?

The lightest solid in the world is a human-made material called aerogel. It contains 99.98% air!

All about liquids

Liquids change shape easily,

but always have the same volume.

You could say liquids are a bit more easygoing than solids. The particles that make up a liquid are connected more loosely than in a solid, and in a more random arrangement. This lets the particles jiggle past each other, so a liquid can flow.

> I just go with the flow, man...

Fixed volume

Although liquids don't have a fixed shape, they do have a fixed volume. A liquid will take up the same amount of space even if the container is changed.

— 250 ml

— 200

— 150

— 100

— 50

75 ml

75 ml

Particles in a liquid have looser bonds than in a solid.

The amount of liquid is the same, but the shape is different.

Liquid properties

Like solids, liquids can have different textures and properties. Some flow more easily than others. Water flows more easily than thick, sticky honey, for example. The word for this is **viscosity**.

That's heavy, dude

Some liquids are denser than others. A very **dense** liquid is heavy, so if you put it in a container with a less dense liquid, they form layers. The heavier, denser liquid will go to the bottom, and the lighter one will go on top. You can see this happen when oil is spilled on wet ground. The oil floats on top of the water, and light refracts through it, creating a rainbow.

👍 Give it a try!

Make a groovy, shakable liquid density column. You'll need a jug, water, vegetable oil, rubbing **alcohol** (70% or 91%), natural sea salt, food coloring (green is good), and a clear plastic bottle or jar with a lid.

First, mix water and salt together in the jug. Keep adding salt and mixing until new salt added won't **dissolve**.

Pour some of this salty water into the clear bottle until it is one-third full. Next, add oil until it is two-thirds full. Finally, pour the alcohol into the bottle until it is nearly full.

Add a few drops of food coloring to the bottle, and shake. The three layers should mix together. But what happens when you set the bottle down?

Shake... and settle

All about gases

Gases have no fixed volume and spread out to fill any space.

Gases are the crazy ones of the bunch. Their particles are not connected, so they whiz about in all directions, full of **energy**. Because of this, a gas will always expand to fill a space.

Particles in a gas are very spread out and can move in all directions.

I'm a laughing gas!

Feel the flow

Gases can flow very easily. Wind is a flow of gas. Fans and hair dryers create gas flows to do work like cooling us down or drying things out.

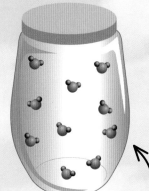

No fixed volume

Unlike solids and liquids, gases don't have a fixed volume. A small amount of gas put into a big container will simply spread out to fill the container. Gases can also be **compressed** very easily.

Did you know?

Gases are all around us, all the time, but most of them are invisible and have no smell.

Hot air in the balloon is lighter than the air outside.

Feel the heat

Heating a material up gives more energy to its particles. The particles in a hot gas will whiz around with even more speed and energy than when cold. This makes the gas spread out further, or increase in volume. Because the particles are spread out further, a hot gas is also less dense and less heavy than a cold gas. This is how hot air balloons work—by making the air in the balloon lighter than the air outside.

How do we get down?

Give it a try!

See how temperature affects the volume of a gas. You will need a balloon, a sewing tape measure, pen and paper, and a freezer.

Blow up the balloon and tie it off. Measure around it at its fattest point.

Record the size of your balloon, then put it in the freezer for two hours.

Now, remove your balloon and immediately measure around it again. What do you notice?

2 HOURS

Melting and Freezing

A solid melts when it warms into a liquid.
A liquid freezes when it cools into solid.

We know that by heating or cooling many materials it is possible to change their states. A solid that is heated up goes soft and loses its fixed shape. It melts or turns into a liquid. A liquid that is cooled down **freezes** into a solid.

Heat energy from the Sun

It's all about the energy

The reason solids melt is because heating matter gives extra energy to the particles. While the atoms have less energy, they stay fairly still, but adding energy makes them jiggle around more and more. Finally the extra energy makes the strong bonds between the particles break down, and the particles can move more freely.

The point at which a solid turns to a liquid is called its melting point.

Am I melting, or just sweating?

Frozen solid

Freezing is the same process as melting, but in reverse. As liquid is cooled, heat energy is taken away, and the particles move around less. Eventually they stay still and form a fixed shape. The temperature at which this happens is called the **freezing point.**

Riddle me this!

If the freezing point of water is 32 °F (0 °C), what is water's melting point?

Answer on page 28.

Hot enough to melt?

It seems odd when you first think about it, but most metals are frozen when at room temperature! For example, the metal aluminum melts at 1,220 °F (660 °C), so at room temperature, which is about 68 °F (20 °C), aluminum is in its solid, frozen state. In contrast, sunflower oil has a melting point of 1 °F (-17 °C), so it is liquid at room temperature.

Evaporating, boiling, and condensing

Liquids evaporate or boil to become a gas. Gases **condense** into a liquid.

Heating and cooling can also change liquids to gases and back again. Just like with melting and freezing, it's all to do with how much energy the atoms have and how much they whiz around.

Boiling

The most dramatic way a liquid becomes a gas is if it **boils**. This is when a liquid is heated to a high temperature, and the particles absorb so much energy that bubbles form throughout the liquid as the whole body turns into a gas at once. The temperature that this happens at is called the **boiling point**.

The boiling point of water is 212 °F (100 °C).

POP QUIZ!

Which of these three things would NOT make a puddle of water **evaporate** faster:

a) Sunny weather

b) Windy weather

c) Humid weather

Answer on page 28.

Cool it!

Our bodies use evaporation to cool us down. Heat energy is carried away from our bodies by our sweat changing from a liquid to a gas.

Gasp, now I need to drink some water!

Evaporation

A liquid doesn't have to boil to become a gas. It can **evaporate** into a gas at cooler temperatures too, but the difference is evaporation only happens at the liquid's surface. Think of the steam rising from a hot cup of tea. At the liquid's surface, the particles are only being held on to the other particles from one side. As a result, it's easier for them to break away and float off as a gas.

Condensation

The opposite of evaporation is **condensation**. This is when particles of a gas lose energy and reform into a liquid. You can see this happen when you breathe onto a cold window or take a cold can out of the fridge. The water vapor in the air is cooled by touching the cold can, and it forms droplets of liquid.

THE WATER CYCLE

Water on Earth is constantly changing from a liquid to a gas and back again.

Water is an unusual material. At the temperatures we normally experience on Earth, most materials are either a solid, liquid, or gas, and generally stay that way. Water is an exception because we regularly find water in all three states: frozen as ice, as a liquid we can drink, or as vapor in the air.

Life giver

The **water cycle** (steps 1–3 in this picture) supports most life on Earth. It provides fresh water, which plants rely on to grow. Plants feed animals (including humans) who also drink the fresh water from the lakes and rivers.

1

Water from oceans and lakes evaporates into the sky to form clouds of water vapor (a gas).

Did you know?

70% of the Earth's surface is covered with water, but 97% of that is salt water in the oceans that we cannot drink.

2

Clouds rise into cold air, causing the vapor to condense into liquid rain.

3

Rain falls onto the land, and runs into lakes and the ocean. The cycle begins again.

Give it a try!

Make your own mini model of the water cycle. You'll need a large metal or plastic bowl, plastic wrap, a mug, a long piece of string or large rubber band, a small weight such as a small stone or pencil sharpener, and some water.

Fill the large bowl with water until it is about a quarter full. Place the mug in the center of the bowl in the water, but make sure the mug is dry on the inside.

Cover the top of the bowl with plastic wrap, and hold it in place with string or the rubber band. Put the small weight directly in the center of the plastic wrap, so it makes a small dip in the plastic over the mug.

Put the bowl in a sunny spot outside and leave it there for about an hour, then move it carefully into the shade. What do you see? Read about it on page 29.

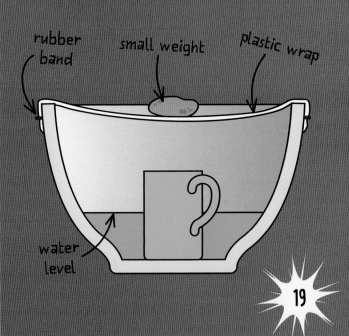

rubber band   small weight   plastic wrap

water level

WHAT is a MIXTURE?

When materials are combined together, they make a mixture.

Mixtures can be solids, liquids, or gases. Most of the objects we find in our day-to-day lives are made up of different materials mixed together.

A mixed picture

Sometimes a mixture is obvious because the bits of each material are big enough to see. Think of a scoop of rocky road ice cream—the bits of cookie, marshmallow, and chocolate are all different materials, so the mixture is easily visible.

I have conducted rigorous scientific tests, and analysis shows this cake IS a mixture.

Scientific analysis tells me this salty water tastes gross!

Invisible ingredients

It's not always obvious just from looking if something is a mixture. Salt water, for example, doesn't look like a mixture because you can't see the separate molecules of salt and water.

A mix of mixtures

Mixtures come in two main types, which have the fancy names of heterogeneous mixtures and homogeneous mixtures.

A HETEROGENEOUS MIXTURE

is a mixture like rocky road ice cream — the different bits are not evenly spread. Other examples of this type of mixture are noodle soup, salad, and chocolate chip cookies.

In a HOMOGENEOUS MIXTURE

like salt water, the bits are evenly distributed. These sorts of mixtures are also called **solutions**. Examples are vinegar and juice.

Does it dissolve?

You can make a solution by dissolving one material in another, such as sugar in tea. If a material dissolves in liquid to make a solution, we say it is **soluble**. If it doesn't dissolve, like sand in water, we say it is **insoluble**.

I told you before, I don't take sugar in my tea!

POP QUIZ!

Decide whether each of these things is a homogeneous mixture or a heterogeneous mixture.

a) Pizza   b) Sugar syrup   c) Soil

Answer on page 29.

SEPARATING MIXTURES

Mixtures can be separated using filtration or distillation.

Mixtures are often useful or necessary, but sometimes we need to separate the different materials in a mixture. How we do this depends on the type of mixture we want to separate.

Simple filters

Sometimes a mixture is quite easy to separate. Think about when you boil a saucepan of peas in water. When the peas are ready, you pour the mixture of peas and water through a colander or sieve. This is a form of **filtration**. The sieve is a filter—it only lets the water through and keeps the peas behind.

Filter

Separate solids

Filtration can be used for other mixtures too. A mixture of solids, such as sand and pebbles, can be poured through a sieve so the larger pebbles are held behind. Sometimes it is necessary to use a filter with very small gaps, like a piece of filter paper. Filter paper will let water pass, but can stop tiny solids like grains of sand.

Solution: distillation!

Filtration doesn't work with solutions like sugar water where the molecules are spread throughout the mixture and are too small to be filtered. To separate a solution we use a process called **distillation**. Distillation works by evaporating the water and leaving the dissolved material (such as sugar) behind.

Riddle me this!

Think about what you know about different liquids' boiling points. Do you think it is possible to separate a mixture of liquids, such as water and alcohol? How could you do it?

Answer on page 29.

2. Only the water evaporates

3. The water cools and condenses again

Mixture

1. The mixture is heated

HA HA, I have the solution!

IRREVERSIBLE CHANGES

Changes in some materials cannot be undone.

Not every material is like water—able to change between the three different states of matter. While some materials can melt and refreeze over and over again, some material changes can only happen once. These are called irreversible changes.

What's cookin'?

Think about frying an egg in a pan: it starts off as a gloopy liquid, then turns into a solid when it is cooked. But cooling it down doesn't turn it back into a raw egg again. This is because heating it has caused chemical changes inside it that cannot be undone.

Feel the burn

Burning is also a type of irreversible change. Heating wood creates smoke and ash, which cannot be changed back into wood.

EYE SPY!

The eggs have cooked and the wood has burned. But can you spot any other irreversible changes in this picture?

Answer on page 29.

Chemical combinations

Irreversible changes don't just come from heating materials—mixing substances can cause irreversible changes too. For example, mixing baking soda with an acid, such as vinegar, releases bubbles of carbon dioxide that cannot be turned back into baking soda and vinegar again.

Give it a try!

Be a rocket scientist! You'll need a 17-ounce (500 ml) plastic bottle and a cork or rubber stopper that fits it, duct tape, three pencils, white vinegar, a tissue, and some baking soda.

Tape the three pencils to the bottle so they create "legs," with the bottle neck pointing downwards. Then turn the bottle upright and half fill it with vinegar.

Peel your tissue's layers apart so you are left with a single layer. Spoon a heaped tablespoon of baking soda onto it. Gently wrap the tissue up around the powder into a slim package.

GO OUTSIDE! Now put the tissue full of baking soda into the bottle, immediately shove the stopper into the top, give the bottle one hard shake, and then stand the rocket upright on the pencil legs. Whoosh!

What change has happened here?

Answer on page 29.

tape

pencil legs

tissue

...3, 2, 1
BLAST OFF!

stopper

25

THE FUTURE OF MATERIALS

Scientists are always developing new types of materials.

Throughout history, from the Stone Age to the modern era of plastics, humankind's use and understanding of materials has transformed how we live our lives. What new materials will change our lives next?

Would you wear spider silk pants?

CHEMICAL COPYCATS

Nature itself has created some of the most impressive materials on the planet, such as spider silk. A spider's web is stronger than steel at the same thickness, and can stretch up to five times without breaking. Scientists have been working on copying spider silk to make this incredible material synthetically.

METAL FOAM

We use plastic foam such as **polystyrene** for packaging because it is light and absorbs energy. But how about metal foam? This new material is super light, but also super strong. In fact, it behaves a lot like human bone. New bone cells can grow around it, so it can be used as a medical implant within a skeleton.

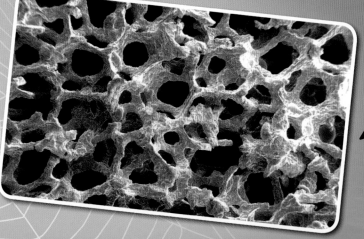

metal foam

GREAT GRAPHENE

Perhaps the biggest advance in material science since the invention of plastic has been the development of graphene. This amazing material is just one atom thick! It is the strongest, lightest, best electricity-conducting material ever created. A sheet the size of a football field would weigh less than 1 ounce (1 g)!

CRACKLESS CONCRETE?

Concrete is the world's most widely-used building material. It is cheap, strong, and can be shaped into whatever design you choose. But over time, heat and rainwater cause cracks. Enter self-healing concrete! Designed by Dutch scientists, it contains limestone-producing bacteria that are activated when rainwater seeps into the structure, filling the cracks up again.

Concrete buildings like this temple could fix themselves!

Did you know?

Scientists who investigate the properties of materials are called materials scientists.

And the answer is...

Page 5 **Riddle me this:** Buildings in earthquake-prone areas will often have flexible materials, such as rubber, in their foundations. These squishy materials can absorb the forces from the earthquake rather than transferring them to the building, which might then crack and fall.

Page 6

Pop quiz: The answer is c), oil is a liquid.

Page 15

Riddle me this: If the freezing point of water is 32 °F (0 °C), then the melting point is ... also 32 °F (0 °C)! It's simply that freezing happens when a material is cooling down, and melting happens when a material is warming up.

Page 16

Pop quiz: The answer is c), humid weather would NOT make a puddle evaporate faster. Wind evaporates puddles by carrying away air that has become full of water vapor, replacing it with dry air that can hold more water molecules.

Page 19

Give it a try: You should see drops of water condensing on the plastic wrap. These then drop as "rain" into the mug.

Page 21

Pop quiz: a) pizza and c) soil are heterogeneous mixtures. b) sugar syrup is a homogeneous mixture.

Page 23

Riddle me this: One way to separate liquids is by making use of their different boiling points. Alcohol has a lower boiling point than water, so if the two are mixed together you can heat the mixture and the alcohol will evaporate first. The alcohol vapor can then be collected, cooled and condensed back into a liquid. Ta da! You have separated the water and the alcohol.

Page 24

Eye spy: The fireworks and the rusty can are both examples of irreversible chemical changes. Rusting is an irreversible chemical change. Certain metals will rust when they come into contact with water and oxygen.

Page 25

Give it a try: By mixing the vinegar and baking soda, a chemical reaction has taken place and a new material, carbon dioxide gas, has been created.

Glossary

Alcohol A colorless flammable liquid

Atom A tiny building block that everything in the universe is made of

Boil When a liquid gets so hot it turns into a gas, with bubbles forming throughout

Boiling point The temperature at which a particular liquid starts to boil

Burn A chemical change where a material breaks down because of heat

Compress When something is squashed together, making it smaller

Condensation The process where a gas cools and becomes a liquid

Dense When the particles of a material are closely packed together

Dissolve When a solid mixes with a liquid completely so it becomes part of the liquid

Distillation A process for separating out mixtures by evaporating liquid

Energy The ability or power to do work

Evaporate Changing from a liquid to a gas at a lower temperature than the boiling point

Filtration Separating mixtures by passing them through a filter, which keeps one or more parts of the mixture behind

Freeze When a liquid turns into a solid

Freezing point The temperature at which a particular liquid turns into a solid

Gas A material that has no fixed volume or shape, such as air. One of the three main states of matter

Insoluble Will not dissolve when put into a liquid

Irreversible Cannot be undone

Liquid A material that has a fixed volume and can flow, such as water. One of the three main states of matter

Material A particular type of matter, or stuff

Matter The word for all physical "stuff" in the universe

Melt When a solid turns into a liquid

Melting point The temperature at which a particular solid turns into a liquid

Mixture When materials are combined together

Molecule A groups of atoms that have joined up

Plasma The fourth, very rare, state of matter

Polystyrene A type of plastic used to make foam packaging

Powder A material made of lots of tiny little bits of a solid

Property A characteristic of a material, such as being hard or soft, or being able to conduct electricity

Solid A material with a fixed shape, such as ice. One of the three main states of matter

Soluble Will dissolve if put into a liquid such as water

Solution A mixture where one of the substances dissolves in the other

State (of matter) One of the forms that matter can exist in: solid, liquid, gas, or occasionally plasma

Viscosity How runny a liquid is

Volume How much space a material fills up

Water cycle The movement of water on Earth between the air, the land, and the ocean

Further Information

Books

Materials
Sally Hewitt
Franklin Watts, 2012

Matter
Peter Riley
PowerKids Press, 2017

Materials and Properties
Peter Riley
Franklin Watts, 2015

Websites

Check out this website for fun experiments to do at home.
www.exploratorium.edu/snacks/subject/materials-matter

Learn more about states of matter here!
www.explainthatstuff.com/states-of-matter.html

Index

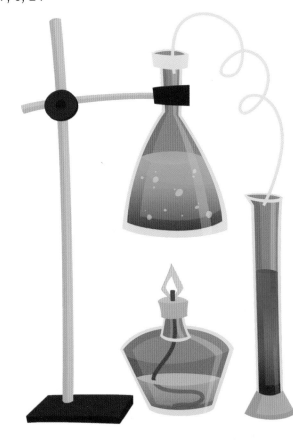